PAULA UMANA

40 GIFTS OF HOPE

Encouragement in times of sickness and suffering

Prologue by Glenda Umaña

© Paula Umana, 2021

First edition: July, 2021

Book cover design: Priscila Coto

Design and layout: Luciana Perera

ISBN: 9798536764619

Important note from the author:

The reader is urged to consult local medical sources and use good judgment when making a decision about his or her health. The purpose of this book is not to give medical advice or diagnosis or to suggest treatments.

For those who have
an illness and are suffering

My profound thanks to the people who opened their hearts to me and told the experiences reflected here.

My infinite gratitude for the unconditional support I have received from my pillars: Marie, Clara, Felicitée, Ana Cecilia, and Charles; and from Serge, my husband and adventure partner. To my parents and family, thank you for all the prayers and for being by my side in the good and the bad.

Thanks to the dedication of the people who helped to make this project, which seeks to be a ray of light in adversity, a reality.

Paula Umana

Contents

Prologue

A neurological illness left Paula, the youngest of my six siblings, immobile in bed and with the anguish of not being able to raise her children. In our immediate family, we had never experienced an illness requiring so many hospitalizations, treatments, and countless moments of uncertainty. Nobody is exempt from suffering and the health difficulties in life, some more serious than others, but what our family had to live through for a long time left us with a feeling of family unity and a positive attitude which will leave a legacy for many generations. As the years pass, Paula gives us an example of courage, perseverance, and a faith so profound that it can only come from the supernatural power of God.

This experience brought her an understanding of the limitations, fear, and frustrations of many ill patients. The substantial changes in her way of living and in her own family were not in vain because she discovered that the path toward recovery is full of obstacles but also miracles. With each experience she realized that she had a mission beyond telling her own story and how God manifested and glorified in every improvement and advancement.

Just as she had a great need for it, Paula recognized that patients and their families are in need of a tool which generates inner strength, visualization, patience, acceptance, and peace. This is why Paula gave herself the task of interviewing various people who found comfort during their suffering by surrendering at the feet of Jesus.

If you are going through a confusing or critical medical diagnosis, if you are suffering from physical pain, if you are in the midst of a treatment in which there is no certainty, if the person who you most love is bedridden and you feel that your physical as well as your emotional strength is weakening, if you have received a death sentence, this devotional is for you.

In these short stories the experiences of various patients are related and accompanied by a teaching and a concrete action so readers may apply them to their own experiences.

This book is not a magical solution for your sufferings or a guaranteed miracle. The purpose is for you to know there are people who may understand what you are going through and can offer their moral support so you can accept your situation, get up, and keep going.

Glenda Umaña
President of Glenda Umaña Communications
CNN en Español Anchor 1997-2014

Introduction

The life of Paula is an example of perseverance and overcoming adversity through personal effort and profound Christian faith.

Born in Costa Rica, Paula was the number one tennis player in her country and Central America in the 1990's; she featured and ranked in the Women's Tennis Association (WTA).

In 2015, a few months after giving birth to her fifth child in Atlanta, Georgia, United States, Paula became quadriplegic due to a neurological disorder known as Chronic Inflammatory Demyelinating Polyneuropathy.

When she was admitted to the Shepherd Center, a hospital specializing in medical treatment and rehabilitation for people with spinal cord injury and other neuromuscular conditions, she realized in order to relieve the emotional suffering which accompanied her physical pain, she needed a message of hope from people who crossed through adverse circumstances similar to her own. Having found no such resource, Paula set out to write this collection to help and inspire others who would go through similar circumstances.

After hundreds of prayers, pilgrimages to shrines, the generosity of many people, and her personal strength, Paula recovered her physical mobility and continues on her path to improvement day by day. Her certainty that the power of her faith helped in her recovery led her to establish her athletic academy, Coach Paula Tennis, and present motivational speeches.

For almost two decades, Paula, a devout Catholic, and her husband, Serge Sautre, a French chiropractor, have lived with their five children in Atlanta.

The experiences told in this work are displays of empathy from their protagonists, who seek to reach the hearts of the sick and provide a means to manage the grief with prayers and teachings.

Physical weakness is accompanied with emotional fragility, and, at times, it is difficult for us to accept guidance despite how helpful it may be. These short stories are a way of telling the reader they are not alone, and with time, it is Paula's sincere desire that the messages of hope, perseverance, faith, and dedication will resonate with the reader and help them on their road to recovery, making them eternally grateful. She encourages you to make the most of them.

> *Blessed be the crisis that made you grow, the fall that made you look up to heaven, the problem that made you seek God.*
>
> — **Padre Pio**

These stories are truly gifts on my 'down' days. Taking only a few minutes to read but inspiring all day long. The brief backgrounds remind me there are many types of suffering, some harder than my own. My favorite part is the practical advice from others like me that allows me to focus on a positive thing to help me that day.

Marianne Gregory, mother of six, diagnosed with stage IV cancer in 2015.

When I was six years old in my native country, El Salvador, I was hit by a car in front of my house.

The doctors gave no hope. I was on the verge of death and suffered a whole year in bed without walking, experiencing the pain and frustration of not being able to play like the other children. My parents clung to a great resource: they prayed the Ave Maria day and night, fervently asking the Virgin of Guadalupe to intercede to her son Jesus for a miracle.

One year after the accident and my recovery, my parents took me by car from El Salvador to the Sanctuary of the Virgin of Guadalupe in Mexico. For five years they drove in the middle of the war years and I brought flowers to thank the Virgin of Guadalupe for the miracle of my recovery and complete healing.

Today 44 years later I have no sequel to the accident!
Pray fervently to the Virgin of Guadalupe!

– **Claudia Robles-Lehmann**

PART ONE

 "Listen to instruction and become wise; do not reject it!"

Proverbs 8 : 33

Heed Those Who Have Suffered

March 2015 and I was in a hospital bed facing the great challenge of my life, a neurological disorder called Chronic Inflammatory Demyelinating Polyneuropathy, or CIDP.

CIDP paralyzed my body, and my mind and spirit were fearful and frustrated. One day Wayne, a psychotherapist from the hospital, came to see me. I shared all of my concerns with him. He listened to me, offered me psychological support, and left.

As I closed the door, I felt that Wayne did not understand what was happening to me. Perhaps he was a great professional, but as he walked out of the room on two healthy legs, he left a devastated person who had lost the use of her own legs. Why should I believe his words? How could he understand what I was going through?

Hours later, I received a visit from the person in charge of the hospital's emotional support group. Minna came to my room in a wheelchair and told me that she had been in a car accident ten years earlier. "My husband died in the accident. I survived, but my legs were left paralyzed. Now I am in charge of offering therapy to patients, and my new husband, Wayne, is also a psychotherapist at this hospital," she said.

Minna's words shocked me, and I changed my perception about Wayne. From then on, I began to listen to everything Wayne had to say because I now knew that he did understand what I was going through and could empathize with the suffering of a person with paraplegia.

I learned that when those who have suffered themselves speak to the ill or to the ailing, they offer great hope to the hearts of those who need it most.

Paula Umana

Take a chance

This story is an empathy tool for people going through a period of suffering, illness, and physical and emotional challenges. Heed the advice of people who experienced suffering similar to the one you have.

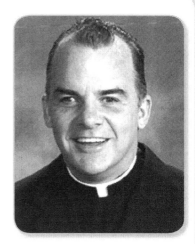

Wow! Paula, our author, has been given a beautiful spiritual vision. As a Catholic priest, totally blind for 90% of my life, I am nourished by the deep stories in these pages, and intend to draw upon them in many upcoming missions and retreats.

40 Gifts of Hope reminds us of God's mysterious plan and the beauty discovered by the people who trust in Him despite all odds. If anyone needs hope in the face of hardship, Paula's story along with the many others shared in this book will remind us of God's piercing goodness and our vocation to trust in Him, permitting God to reveal deeper beauty and meaning in the midst of shadows.

— Rev. Michael Joly

" Forty years after facing leukemia, José is a healthy athlete and professional tennis coach. "

José, I love you

In 1979, I was an 18-year-old Costa Rican student who, full of dreams, began his university career in the state of Oregon, United States.

I stood out as a dedicated athlete. My routine was to go for a run every morning, but one day I felt uncommonly weak.

Since it was an abnormal feeling, I went to the university infirmary. They told me it was a simple cold, and they gave me medication. However, the discomfort got worse, and my weakness increased. For this reason, a week later, I returned to the infirmary, and they referred me to a private clinic where I had a bone marrow examination.

Within hours, a doctor told me that I had Acute Myelogenous Leukemia and that I should be admitted to the hospital immediately for chemotherapy treatment.

I felt perplexed. I was in a country that was not mine, and doctors diagnosed me with a disease I had never heard about. When doctors explained this type of leukemia to me, I thought, "I'm going to die, this is cancer in my blood, and there is no cure for this acute leukemia."

In addition to the diagnosis, something extraordinary happened that day. After communicating with my mother in Costa Rica, I received a call from my father, a very busy man absorbed in his work.

My father told me a phrase that I had not heard in eighteen years: "José, I love you." I started crying because it was the sweetest expression I had ever heard from him.

Those words gave me the strength to fight for my life. My whole family's support and the letters my friends sent me helped face the situation and not give up.

José Naranjo, president of Orange Tennis Academy

Forty years after facing leukemia, José is a healthy athlete and professional tennis coach.

"*My father told me a phrase that I had not heard in eighteen years: "José, I love you."*"

Act now!

A simple phone call saying I love you to a person with an illness can work miracles. Whom are you going to call today?

"Being able to do things for myself makes me feel strong and, with a little help, I can achieve my goals."

– Beau Broten

Don't be Shy

Because I was premature, I was born blind in my left eye and had very low vision in my right eye. Since I can remember, I was told that I would never be able to see like everybody else.

Using magnification devices, I was able to go to school but reading and writing were challenging for me. I had to use a cane to walk. Despite my limitations, I was able to have a wonderful childhood. I especially loved playing with kids in my Valley Park neighborhood in Minneapolis.

However, when I was a teenager, I became incredibly angry. I was excluded from a lot of activities because of my limitations. I was not able to do simple things, like just live simply in the house I wanted to live in. I realized that I was never going to be able to drive a car or be as independent as my peers. It was difficult to accept my circumstances.

At that time public transportation was not an option for me. My parents, brothers, and friends from church would drive me to my activities. I really started to feel better as I grew up, and I developed great friendships through my church's youth group. Unfortunately, in my late twenties and early thirties, my right eye got worse and I eventually became totally blind.

It was only with the help of my family and friends that I was able to continue with school and work. I went to college and got a bachelor's degree in finance and accounting. My first job was with the Navy doing office work.

Now after 15 years of being blind, I have learned to share my story with other groups of blind people. This has empowered me. I realize I can do everything I ever wanted to do with just a little help.

I currently have a great job working for the IRS. I am able to take trains, buses and airplanes. I go to church every Sunday and I am overall an incredibly happy person. I work a lot so that I can afford the activities I love. My favorite outdoor activities are rock climbing and river rafting. I also enjoy going to the professional football and basketball games in my current city, Atlanta. Every year, I go to several Atlanta Falcons football games and all the Atlanta Hawks basketball games. This has allowed me to meet a lot of amazing people and learn so much.

Every time I arrive in a new place and I do not know where to go, I always ask for help. Most of the time I count on the generous cooperation of those present. Be worth of myself makes me feel strong and, with a little help, I can achieve my goals.

Beau Broten, Atlanta, United States

The best advice that Beau Broten can give if you are ill and suffering:

1. God loves you. He has a purpose for you. You are here for a reason.

2. Do not be shy. Ask for help when you need it. 99% of people will help you.

3. Remember that there are always people out there who love you.

4. Find a way to do outdoor activities.

5. Put some music on and talk to God. Tell him everything.

An Empowered Team

When one is in a difficult situation or facing illness, it is vital to ask for help. But above all, it is indispensable to ask for prayers.

As I previously explained, a neurological disorder had left me immobile. The only thing I could do was talk. Despite my poor physical condition, I asked myself: "How is it possible to feel so much peace and joy in the middle of the storm?" It was then that I realized that people who love me were praying for me. Those prayers gave me the strength and courage to face hardship.

I am sure my inner peace was due to hundreds of people interceding for me. Why did I feel calm despite my physical pain when nothing seemed to be right in my life? I know in my heart that the answer can only be explained by the special graces of the Holy Spirit and by the prayers that gave me incredible comfort.

We are not alone in difficult times. Trials often come in our lives so that we can fulfill God's will by helping each other carry our burdens.

Having people who support us and help us overcome adversity can completely change the process we go through and the outcome.

Paula Umana

Therefore, confess your sins to one another and pray for one another, that you may be healed. The fervent prayer of a righteous person is very powerful.

James 5: 16

Ask for prayer

Make a list of friends and family who are close to God and humbly ask them to pray for you.

_____

_____

_____

" *So confess your sins to one another and pray for one another, that to be cured; the heartfelt prayer of someone upright works very powerfully.* "

James 5:16

"*In your difficult times use the resource of calling your mother. But remember if you don't have your own mom, pray and talk to the Virgin Mary, mother of Jesus. She will intercede for you and help you in difficult times.*"

– Charlene O'Brien

"It is going to be okay"

I never thought of the power my mother's words would have to help me cope with my physical and emotional illnesses. Thanks to her I know that the recitation of the Rosary and the novena to the Virgin Mary ease my afflictions.

I was 25 when I thought my life had come to an end. I was diagnosed with multiple sclerosis weeks after the first symptoms such as numbness of the face, double vision, speech disorder and balance problems appeared.

I collapsed on the floor, with the phone in my hands and cried. I did not want to share this horrible news with my boyfriend or my roommates, so I ran up to my room and called my mom. My mom and I decided to keep my diagnosis a secret. She just kept telling me that "it is going to be okay". She didn't say it would be easy, or that my life hadn't changed, but she said it would be okay. She knew that worrying would only make things worse. I learned from my very devout mom that faith and powerful prayers like the Rosary and Novena to the most Blessed Mother would help.

I eventually moved to Atlanta, Georgia, where I joined the Cathedral of Christ the King and met my husband, Brian. Brian has been a very supportive husband and accepts all of the limitations that MS has put on me.

Since my diagnosis in 1996, the medicines available for MS have drastically improved.

I currently have just one Tysabri infusion each month, and I am humbly proud to say that I am still walking. 26 years after I was sure my life was over, I have a wonderful family and as my mom predicted, everything is going to be ok.

However, these years have not been easy. I struggle with depression and I blame myself for not being the mother/wife/friend that I had always imagined I would be. Some days I am so tired and in so much pain, I forget how blessed I am. On those bad days, I just have to remember to call my mom. She always listens, lets me vent all of my emotions, and reminds me that "it is all going to be okay."

Charlene O'Brien, Atlanta, United States

Call Your Mom

In your difficult times use the resource of calling your mother. But remember if you don't have your own mom as a resource, pray and talk to the Virgin Mary, mother of Jesus. She will intercede for you and help you in difficult times.

> **"**A generous and anonymous person gave me the gift of life when they donated their liver. I am deeply grateful to them.**"**

— Tatiana

Here and Now!

At the age of fifteen, I was diagnosed with Ulcerative Colitis, a chronic inflammatory disease of the large intestine or colon. I learned to cope with the symptoms, studied abroad, and became a successful professional. I also got married, had a wonderful daughter, and built my life in the United States.

Years later, it became difficult for me to do everyday things. Doctors informed me of the need for a liver transplant because my illness had irreversibly damaged my organ due to complications with my disease.

A generous and anonymous person gave me the gift of life when they donated their liver. I am deeply grateful to them.

On the day of the surgery, I took my little girl to school, and when she said goodbye, I was heartbroken and worried. Hours later, I entered the operating room with the scapular given by my mother and the conviction God would bring me through this. Even though the operation lasted ten hours and I lost a lot of blood, it was a success. Weeks after the surgery, I went back to work and began making long-term plans.

A year after the liver transplant, the doctors told me that a colon operation was necessary. It was complicated to accept the news, but my immense faith in God was the strength that kept me going. In addition to my faith and prayers, I sought psychological support and coping mechanisms for this new challenge. I found a peaceful oasis in special moments. Mindfulness helped me enjoy the unique moments that I was experiencing.

I learned to engage fully in conversations with friends, focus on my breathing, and even be aware of the sensations under my feet when walking through the garden. Lowering my guard allowed me to cope with my suffering and anxiety. The here and now is, after all, all we have.

I see what I have overcome. Gratefully, I learned to value the inner strength I acquired during difficult moments of my life.

Tatiana

Surrender

Meditate on the here and now using Mindfulness meditation. Feel your breath and live each moment as if it were exceptional. Spend ten minutes writing down thoughts that cross your mind, in any order, even if it doesn't make sense. Empty your mind and fill yourself with inner peace.

Suffering cannot be transformed and changed with an exterior grace, but an interior one.

— Juan Manuel Fernández Piera

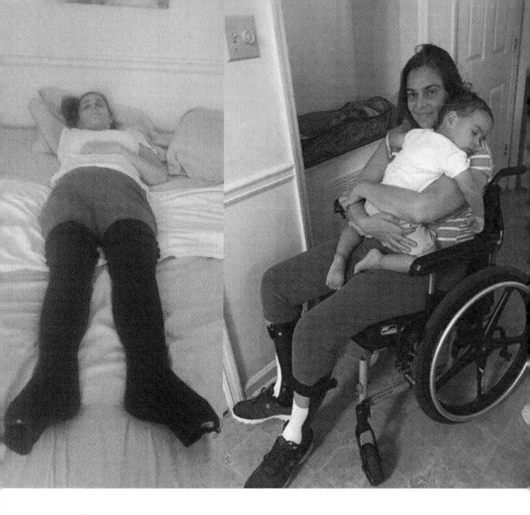

" *Offer your suffering for others, in a state of privilege and purification!* **"**

— **Paula Umana**

I Suffer for You

Prostrated with quadriplegia in a bed, I began to have the terrible and terrifying experience of disability.

When my little daughters came up to ask me to brush their hair or help them close the button on their school skirts, I could not do it. I began to feel a state of emotional torture.

I had to decide how to deal with my new reality. My options were limited. The first option was to take medications for panic and anxiety disorders that my doctors had prescribed. But in my case, this option was isolating me from the family. The second option was to find another way to handle the situation from an emotional point of view.

I received a valuable visit from Father Wilberto Reyes, a priest from Puerto Rico, who told me about the idea of "learning to offer God our suffering for other people or situations."

He told me that suffering has no value if we don't use it for something good. We waste our time crying, complaining, and feeling frustrated, which doesn't have any positive results.

So I put a new plan into practice. I asked for photos and written requests from friends and family for those that were in need of prayer, and I put an image of Jesus of Divine Mercy on the wall in front of me.

This way, every time I felt emotionally tortured, I would read the petitions, look at the photos, and give my suffering for them to God.

When we offer our suffering on behalf of other people, something miraculous happens; we purify ourselves. In pain, we enter a state of privilege where, in due time, God gives us his grace, and we can carry the burden in a sanctifying way and with great peace.

Paula Umana

Put this exercise into practice

Offer your suffering for others in a state of privilege and purification!

Put names and photographs of the people for whom you offer your suffering on your bedroom wall and think of them when you are suffering yourself.

"When we offer our suffering on behalf of other people, something miraculous happens; we purify ourselves. In pain, we enter a state of privilege where, in due time, God gives us his grace, and we can carry the burden in a sanctifying way and with great peace."

– Paula Umana

> **"** When the sun shines I can achieve what I set out to do; no mountain is too high, no problem is too difficult to overcome. **"**

Wilma Rudolph

Don't give up!

I was the best tennis player in Costa Rica. I was preparing to travel to the United States because I had won a scholarship to study and play tennis at Azusa Pacific University in California.

My friends said goodbye to me, and when we were returning to our houses, an accident happened that changed my destiny. The driver of the car I was in tried to dodge another vehicle, hit the fence at the edge of the freeway, and I was thrown out the window. I was left in a coma for more than a week. Doctors did not expect me to live.

Upon awakening from the coma, I learned that I had a punctured lung, multiple fractures, a brain clot, and a severe thoracic spinal cord injury that left me in a wheelchair. The skin on my back was raw, and the pain was brutal. It took four people to bathe me. I was scared, and my mind was full of doubts.

Despite the pain and sadness, I decided to fight for my recovery, thanks to my family's support. I started to push myself to try, little by little, to fend for myself and try to have new experiences on my own.

The first time I saw something different in a long time was when my father forced me to go for a walk with my family in the mountains of Monteverde. He pushed me because I felt weak, upset, and angry. He dragged me up the hill until we reached a waterfall that, when contemplating it, made me feel like myself again and gave me the strength to strive and desire new experiences such as this one that was such an inspiration to me.

On another occasion, my father took me to play tennis in an adapted wheelchair. I admit that it was horrible the first time, but I felt the same feeling I had before my injury, like when I played on the courts after several practices. I found my passion once more.

Today, after much sacrifice and tenacity, I am the best-adapted tennis player in Central America and number 49 in the world. I'm also part of a wheelchair basketball team, exercising and training five hours a day. In addition, I founded Tennis on Wheels, an organization dedicated to helping the disabled play tennis. I feel fulfilled, full of challenges, and happy.

José Pablo Gil, founder of Tennis On Wheels

Don't stay in the past

Accept the challenge of playing sports and exploring activities in which you will discover new ways to challenge yourself, get exercise, and have fun.

During radiation, I closed my eyes and visualized myself healthy. I would say to myself, "I'm not going to get the side effects of that radiation," and I would envision the radiation killing all the cancer cells in my body.

– José Naranjo,

President of Orange Tennis Academy

Aranjuez Concert

In the basement of the Fred Hutchinson Cancer Research Center in Seattle, I prepared for six days of full-body cobalt bomb radiation. The nurse came to lead me to the therapy room. A sign on a gray door read "Radiation: Do Not Enter."

The place was cold. It had two orange columns at both ends and a table in the center. In one corner, there was an all-glass room where technicians operated instruments to apply radiation.

Every day I would lie on the table, and next to me, I had a cassette with the music from the "Concert of Aranjuez." It was the favorite piece of Héctor, my brother and spinal cord donor. As the radiation sessions began, I was carried away by the melody.

During radiation, I closed my eyes and visualized myself healthy. I would say to myself, "I'm not going to get the side effects of that radiation," and I would envision the radiation killing all the cancer cells in my body.

After treatment, I had a challenging but successful bone marrow transplant. I survived!

José Naranjo, President of Orange Tennis Academy

Application

Take a deep breath and ask God to take away your fears.

Apply Jose's teaching in your health situation, with music and visualization.

An Angel Crosses Your Path

My neurological disease is rare. After many months of testing, the doctors finally came to the correct diagnosis: Chronic Inflammatory Demyelinating Polyneuropathy (CIDP).

They invited me to meet people with similar conditions. Once there, I was confused because the other patients came in walking, ordering food at the restaurant, and using cutlery. In contrast, I was in a wheelchair, my legs were frail, and my hands could not even hold a plastic fork.

It caused me a lot of frustration to see other attendees healthier than I was. At the get-together, I met Sandy, who had two canes and splints on her legs. She came up to me and said, "You have to pray a lot and get eight months of immunoglobulin infusions to get on your feet. I was just like you for a year."

It was the best advice I ever got. I trusted Sandy's words, I was patient, and in the sixth month after receiving the infusions, on February 11, the Day of the Virgin of Lourdes, I managed to stand up and take my first step.

Meeting a person with a condition similar to mine filled me with hope and gave me confidence that I would move forward. I suppose people like Sandy appear like angels on our paths. Rejoice and learn from their experiences!

Paula Umana

Prayer

Lord, I ask you to put people who have gone through suffering similar to mine in my path. Please grant me the humility to ask for advice and wisdom to understand. Amen.

Make a list of people who are sick and who can advise you:

_____

_____

_____

PART TWO

"The fear that I felt in those daily fifteen minutes of radiotherapy was so overwhelming, that God enlightened me to imagine that I was in a garden."

– Helen Rosenberg de Barahona

An Oasis Behind the Mask

Several decades ago, sunblock did not exist; when I was young, my friends and I slathered butter or a popular soft drink to tan our skin while enjoying the summer sun. Years passed, and my skin paid the consequences of my youthful ignorance.

I have had many health problems, including Infiltrating Carcinoma on my face. Infiltrative because it is a type of cancer that grows and advances like a robust ivy. I have had operations, transplants, and grafts. After surgery, the doctor ordered twenty-five radiotherapy sessions, which were torture because I had to put on a closed mesh mask that they secured to a treatment table. It was terrible because I suffer from claustrophobia. The fear was so overwhelming, but I felt that God enlightened me in those daily fifteen minutes of therapy, and I began to imagine that I was in a garden.

I imagined fragrant roses, various types of flowers, a stream with turtles and little fish, trees that moved in the breeze, and delicious smells that enveloped me. I saw small birds, butterflies, a rainbow, and Jesus and Mary, to whom I ran to receive a blessing.

As the days passed, I invited family, the sick, the homeless, and those who had prayed for me to my imaginary garden so that they could also receive a blessing. My made-up world was the only way I survived twenty-five sessions inside a mask that terrified me.

Later in life, I was diagnosed with Parkinson's disease. A friend very wisely told me, "You can believe in the diagnosis, but not in the prognosis." I replied, "Yes! I will." I don't know if Parkinson's will ever stop taking control of my body, but what I do know is that God has the last word.

Helen Rosenberg de Barahona, Guatemala

Visualize the garden

If you go through moments of fear, visualize a garden, fill it with all the flowers, sights, smells, and people you care about. Feel the breeze, look around you, and internalize the beauty surrounding you in your imaginary garden. Run to Jesus and Mary to receive a blessing. You will overcome fear and find comfort in the arms of Christ.

"Do not be afraid of pain, let the Holy Spirit do his work on you."

Mother Andrea de Jesus

❝My two pillars remind me every day that no matter how bad the prognosis is, God is God.❞

– Wendy Cruz

Will I Have the Blessing of Being a Mother?

January 2008. I was a young woman, just married, full of health, with many goals and dreams. A month later, I was bedridden, sick, bloated, in pain, and very confused.

My immune system went haywire and caused damage to my kidneys. The inflammation caused an imbalance throughout my body. But that was not all; the doctor warned me that I should dismiss the idea of becoming a mother. It took me a lot to understand that behind so much pain, God has a perfect plan.

Many people prayed for me while the doctors gave me powerful treatments to get my kidneys to react. I remember with particular affection the prayer of a friend who told me, "God will heal you completely so that you can bear witness. One day this will be but a memory, and you will have two children who will be your pillars."

At that moment in time, her declaration sounded more like a joke. What's surprising is that, in due course, everything she told me came true. Six months after treatment, my medical examinations revealed that everything was back to normal.

As my doctor had warned me, the medications affected my ability to get pregnant, but I managed to deliver my two children with a specialist's help. My two pillars remind me every day that no matter how bad the prognosis is, God is God.

In our eyes, it seems that injustice or a tragedy is, perhaps, the prelude to a great miracle or even two or three.

Wendy Cruz, journalist

 *Aceptance with Faith allows us to live in peace.*

— **Erika Nahrgang**

Remember

Every time you have fear or doubts, repeat: "Jesus, I trust in you."

A Sign

It was May, and I had already been hospitalized for four months after my diagnosis of CIDP. I became quadriplegic and separated from my five children. One day, I was crying in despair over what was happening to me when I received a phone call from Carolina, my best friend from Costa Rica. Together in prayer we pleaded to God to send us a sign that he had not abandoned me.

The next day, on the occasion of Mother's Day in the United States, the hospital let me go to Sunday Mass. My husband and my friend Violaine took me to the Cathedral of Christ the King in Atlanta, which was packed because of such an important celebration.

At the end of the Mass, the priest stood in front of everyone with a large bouquet and said, "These flowers are only for one mother in this whole parish, and they will be for the mother of the youngest baby."

New mothers began to raise their hands and say their babies' ages. The friend who accompanied me raised her hand and, pointing to me, said that my baby was five months old. The priest told me that I was the winner, and when I turned my head, I saw that a bouquet was approaching me. They placed it on my legs, and everyone in the church began to applaud.

When they gave me the bouquet, something beautiful happened. The request I made to the Lord to send me a sign came to my mind. I felt that God was telling my heart His answer, that among all the mothers, He chose me exclusively to give a gift, assuring me that He cared for me in those difficult moments.

God filled my heart with joy and hope. Thank you, Lord, because whatever the setbacks, you always take care of us. Amen.

Paula Umana

Stop

Make time for God.

Turn everything off around you that could be a distraction.

Talk to God for ten minutes.

Your history, your sufferings, and your miracles are unique; do not compare yourself with others.

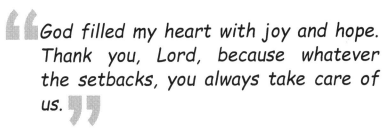

God filled my heart with joy and hope. Thank you, Lord, because whatever the setbacks, you always take care of us.

– Paula Umana

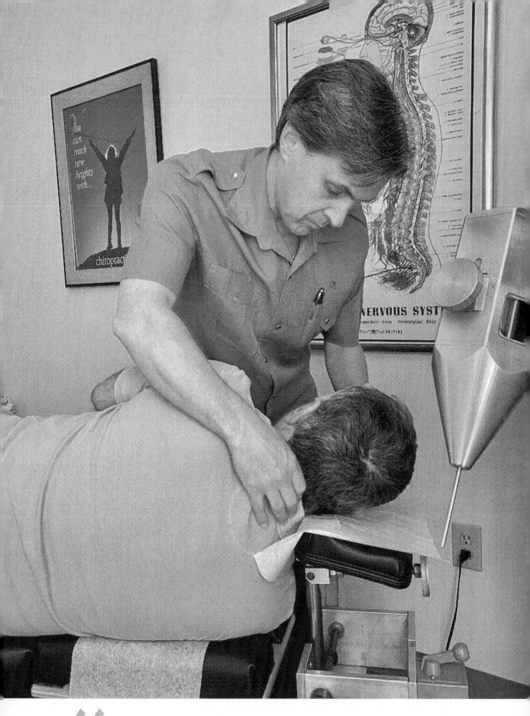

" *The preservation of health is easier than the cure for disease.* "

– B. J. Palmer, D.C.

Vocation and Healing

As Paula's dedicated husband, and as a witness of my wife's suffering, frustration, faithfull acceptance of God's Providence, and healing, I have grown in my understanding of the significant challenges a person with disabilities faces daily.

From my experience, I also know how a patient feels after an automobile accident. Years ago, in my native country of France, this misfortune happened to me for a reason! While it prevented me from participating in a tennis tournament and from enjoying life for a while, months after completing a conventional medical treatment, I was able to play tennis and ice hockey again, but I was not well, until... One of my father's friends, Daniel, suggested visiting a chiropractor in Paris because he emphatically told my parents that I looked crooked.

Chiropractic care took an immediate effect on me, helped my body heal, and I gained confidence again. It ignited my interest for the chiropractic career. I thought about changing my educational path again after starting engineering, then maths and structural sciences, my dad encouraged me to find a job to pay for my chiropractic education and later he supported me to go study chiropractic abroad.

After attending daily Mass, silent retreats in the Benedictine Monastery of Our Lady of Fontgombault, and the spiritual guidance from my high school priest, Father John, I realized that chiropractic was my vocation and responded to that call.

Chiropractic is funded on alignments of the spine (adjustments) to allow the nervous system to improve our body's functions and ultimately relieve some pain and suffering. Chiropractic simply contributes to releasing the healing power of the body God created.

I have seen countless cases like that of Ana, who came to my office on her neurologist's recommendation. The patient had suffered a stroke and was unable to speak clearly. I adjusted the atlas, the first cervical vertebra, and she immediately stood up and began talking. Imagine the happiness, she did not even realize what happened!

Luz, a mother in her forties, came to her appointments with a walker, a wheelchair and a long list of prescription drugs. After an atlas adjustment, she was able to walk, and it transformed her life. Now she practices good, healthy habits.

Salvador, a plumber, father of three with meager resources was about to undergo spinal surgery for a herniated disc after a work injury. With chiropractic care, he improved gradually, healed without surgery and returned to work to support his family.

God blessed me by working with some of the greatest mentors in the profession to develop my talents and encouraged me to always give the best adjustment to each patient regardless of their medical conditions and financial ability to afford care. With more than 25 years in chiropractic, after performing thousands of chiropractic adjustments to the rich and the poor, the elite athlete and the one suffering from disabilities, I know that each person is unique and God created the body with the amazing self healing power of life and a soul that animates that body. My simple conclusion as a chiropractor is that the life experience is better when the spine is in proper alignment, allowing the nervous system to function properly.

My mission is to serve our Lord by serving each patient providing the best chiropractic adjustments I can and encourage each person to adopt healthy living habits.

Dr. Serge Sautre, Chiropractor

Encouragement

Consider reaching a local chiropractor to help you. Receiving chiropractic adjustments regularly, prayers and exercising daily according to your means, may allow you to experience changes and improvements in your health regardless of your limitations, which by the way we all have.

"The power that made the body, heals the body."

— BJ Palmer, DC.

"That power is the power coming out of Christ when the sick bleeding lady touched His garment."

— Sister Brigitte Yengo, Nun, MD, DC

"When your spine is in line, the nervous system functions improve, resulting in better health, mobility and happiness. "

— Serge Sautre, DC

"Chiropractic, like gravity, works whether you believe it or not."

— Sid E. Williams D.C

A Simple Faith

On December 24, 1993, I prayed the Rosary at home, and for the first time, I felt the embrace of the mother of Jesus, who told me, "You are not alone."

Days later, a truck hit my husband; the impact was such that his extremities were broken. When I received the news, my reaction was to say over and over again, "My God, help me."

The doctors allowed me to enter Carlos's emergency operation, and in that room, I felt for the second time the embrace of Jesus mother and her words: "You are not alone."

I took care of my husband for thirteen years. Twenty-four operations later, he went from a person with quadriplegia to having paraplegia. He finally managed to walk with difficulty.

On December 15, 2006, Carlos went into cardiac arrest. I received the news when I was driving my car, and again I received the embrace of the mother of Jesus and her words: "You are not alone."

Carlos was in a vegetative state. The family's hope of seeing him recover disappeared, and I took care of him for another eight years. My husband passed away on December 26, 2014. During those 20 years of illness, pain, and tragedy, I always had peace. Why?

I found peace in a simple phrase: Lord, I accept what is happening, and I place it in your hands.

Vivian Herrera

A simple prayer

Open your heart with humility and declare: Jesus, I receive your embrace. Please, help me. Lord, I accept what is happening and leave it in your hands. Amen.

> *During those 20 years of illness, pain, and tragedy, I always had peace. Why?*
>
> *I found peace in a simple phrase: Lord, I accept what is happening, and I place this in your hands.*

– Vivian Herrera

"Never, never lose hope! God surprises us in beautiful ways!"

– Paula Umana

Our Lady of Lourdes Sent me an Angel

The experts at the Vanderbilt Neuromuscular Disorders Clinic in Tennessee, one of the most prestigious clinics in the United States, had assured me that I would never walk again.

Faced with such a daunting prospect, my eldest daughter, Marie, decided to travel to the Sanctuary of Our Lady of Lourdes to pray for my health. While my daughter pleaded for my well-being in France, I went to a supermarket in the United States. A woman named Angel came up to me and said, "I want to show you what I wear on my legs. I think it can help you." Thus began the miracles.

Angel showed me some leg braces. The devices are known as ExoSym. They cost thousands of dollars and are custom-made in Seattle.

It was then that the other miracle happened. The day my braces arrived, my neighbor, Beatriz, called the clinic in Seattle and paid the bill in full.

Every morning, I wake up full of hope and expectations because near my bed, I have the apparatus I wear on my legs, and I am free. I can walk!

Paula Umana

Cheer up

Never, never lose hope! God surprises us in beautiful ways!
Write down a memory that fills you with hope.

Cling to hope, let yourself be surprised by God and live with joy.

– Pope Francis

I learned that when situations look unpleasant and bleak, God's plan is always better than what we have in mind.

– Cristina Pacheco

There is Hope!

On August 17, I was on my way to the movies when my mother urgently stopped me from going. She told me we had to go to the doctor's office immediately because an analysis revealed the cause of the discomfort that plagued me.

The doctor surprised us with the diagnosis that I had an advanced stage of Lupus, a chronic autoimmune disease, in an advanced stage and I had only two months to live. At just twenty years old, my life was hanging by a thread. It is hard for someone to receive that news at such a young age. You are supposed to have a lifetime ahead of you.

After the diagnosis, I went to the parking lot where I cried and thought about my future. "What will the rest of my life be like? Will I be happy?" I wondered.

The doctor gave me a choice between two treatments. One was a chemotherapy treatment that would be more effective but render me sterile. The other treatment was medication, but I didn't know if it would be as useful. I opted for the pill treatment, which was a very difficult decision. Specialists warned me that when a woman has Lupus, it is challenging to get pregnant.

Seven years have passed since the diagnosis, and now, every August, I celebrate the life and the experience I went through because, although it was not easy, it served a greater good. God had a bigger plan for me: a healthy, happy life and a baby on the way. I learned that when situations look unpleasant and bleak, God's plan is always better than what we have in mind.

It is good for me that I have been afflicted; that I might learn thy statutes. The law of thy mouth is better unto me than thousands of gold and silver. Psalm 119:71-72

Cristina Pacheco

She gave birth to a boy in 2020.

Look at Cristina's photo with her baby, think about your situation, and fill yourself with hope.

Visual exercise

Get photos that remind you of beautiful memories of your life. Transport yourself to that time and place, feel the emotion of that day. Forget about what might have been, enjoy what you have, and be grateful for the happiness you felt.

❝No matter how high the waves are, the Lord is higher. Wait! ... calm will return.**❞**

– Padre Pio

Relieve Your Pent-up Feelings

My life changed when I was 24 years old, and I worked as a highway inspector in Costa Rica.

Once a colleague who worked on the Nandayure - Naranjo beach route fell ill, and the bosses sent me to fill his position. When I was driving on a highway, I lost control of my car, and an accident left me with a fractured spine and a spinal cord injury in the T-9. I ended up paraplegic. Ten years have passed ever since then, and I am in a wheelchair.

The first couple of years after my injury were exhausting. I struggled day and night to regain what I could in body movement and underwent intense physical therapy.

During this crucial time and even today, I give myself the right to cry, and when I weep, the venting helps me feel better and heals wounds in my heart. Little by little, God was showing me my new identity.

Natalia Vindas, architect

The benefits of crying

Take some time to mourn what happened.

Unburden yourself before God with a sincere heart.

After crying, make sure you accomplish your mission.

Jesus, with his unconditional love, accompanies us in our pain.

Prayers and petitions interceded for a miracle to take place in my body, and three years later, I was able to walk again.

— Paula Umana

The Pilgrimage

The Virgin of Los Ángeles is celebrated in Costa Rica every August the 2nd. The streets of the city of Cartago are closed, and more than three million people go on a pilgrimage to the Basilica of Our Lady of Los Angeles. Many sing to God, offer sacrifices and prayers, and thank the mother of Jesus.

In August 2015, forty family members went on a pilgrimage to the Basilica to pray for my health while I was paralyzed and bedridden.

The day after the pilgrimage, I was finally able to sit up for the first time on my own. Imagine being able to move your body after months of lying prostrate in bed. Prayers and petitions interceded for a miracle to take place in my body, and three years later, I was able to walk again.

The mother of Jesus has manifested worldwide: the Virgin of Guadalupe in Mexico, the Virgin of Lourdes in France, Our Lady of Fatima in Portugal, and the Virgin of Los Angeles in Costa Rica.

Paula Umana

Pilgrim

If you have the opportunity to make a pilgrimage, don't think twice. It is a powerful spiritual journey, and the experience is unforgettable. If you want someone to pray for you in Lourdes, France, you can petition directly to the Grotto of Our Lady of Lourdes on the website: www.lourdes-france.org/en/

PART THREE

The Importance of Emotional Support

My meeting with cancer took place a week after my gallbladder surgery. At the follow-up appointment, my surgeon gave me the good news, the lab test results from my surgery were satisfactory; later, the bad news came.

My primary care doctor had called him the night before to share the results of a breast biopsy of mine that she had been waiting for. The surgeon told me that the tests revealed Ductal Carcinoma In Situ (DCIS) stage zero in the left breast.

"It's zero, there is no cancer," I told him. "I said stage zero. I didn't say there was no cancer," he replied. The doctor went on to explain that DCIS occurs when the cells that line the breast milk duct change to cancer cells, but they do not spread outside of the ducts into the surrounding breast tissue.

I remembered reading some articles about women who, after learning the diagnosis, ask, "Why me?" I thought, "Why not me?" After all, my maternal grandmother died of breast cancer and some studies indicate that the abnormal gene can be passed on.

I asked the doctor if I could have the procedure after the holidays because I had an end-of-year trip to my country. He said we had to act quickly because my condition could worsen. The surgery would be a lumpectomy to get the bad cells out, not a removal of the whole breast.

After I left the hospital, I broke down, not for me, but for my family. When I told them about the diagnosis, they were shaken, but they expressed their full support. As a true journalist, I did a full investigation on breast cancer and read an extraordinary amount of articles I found on the web.

The next morning I met Dale, a member of the breast cancer patient support group that the surgeon recommended to me. I think my tears flooded the lady's office. I asked her so many questions that she realized I was very confused because I had an overload of information. I was scared.

She had medical diagrams to explain the diagnosis and she assured me that I was going to return home the same day of the surgery. She explained that a few weeks later I was going to start radiation treatment to the breast.

Dale handed me a booklet with information and said not to read page 32. Of course the first thing I did was to look for the "forbidden" page and she, who was looking out of the corner of her eye, said with a grin: "I don't think you are going to get prostate cancer!"

At the end of our meeting, she told me to calm down, that I was going to be OK and that I should trust the words of a double mastectomy survivor who endured many chemotherapy and radiation treatments. I cried and asked for her forgiveness; I realized that my problem was nothing compared to what she went through.

Days later, I was at the hospital ready for my second surgery in three weeks. When a male nurse was taking me to the operating room, he stopped briefly and there she was. Dale, dressed in a white suit like an angel, walked toward the stretcher, took my hand and said that she was going to be with me during the procedure. Her reassuring words comforted me and I was feeling so grateful that I arrived at the doors of the operating room with a big smile. I recognized the surgeon behind the special glasses and the surgical gown and asked him to sing a song.

After recovering from the general anesthesia, the doctor and Dale told me that the lumpectomy was successful. We had to wait for the lab test results. The surgeon gave me an early Christmas present: I could travel to my country, but first I had to promise that I was going to take good care of myself.

After my return, the radiology experts marked my chest for the daily therapy visits. The doctor in charge informed me that each session was going to be short, that the skin area where I was going to receive the radiation would gradually turn dark, and that after a certain number of weeks, I would feel tired, not from the therapy, but due to the new routine.

During my treatment, I met doctors, nurses, and experts whose empathy helped patients to face breast cancer with confidence, hope, and peace of mind.

After a few years, I received an invitation for a retirement and farewell party in Dale's honor. There were so many people there to wish her well. I never imagined the love and gratitude of so many patients, doctors, nurses, and administrative staff for her. Just as Dale gave me the confidence to face the challenge and helped me to face my fears, my angel also touched the lives of many because she knew first-hand what we had to go through.

Tatyana Heredia, Journalist

Prayer

Lord, I ask you to put the right people in my life so they can help me carry the burden when I need it most. Amen.

Prevention and control

Look for information on general health topics. Read about symptoms and diagnoses. Remember to make an appointment for your mammogram or cancer screening. Better safe than sorry.

"To speak of hope to those who are desperate, it is necessary to share their despair; To wipe a tear from the face of a person who suffers, it is necessary to unite our crying with theirs. Only in this way can our words really be able to give a little hope. And if I can't say words like that, with tears, with pain, silence is better; the caress, the gesture and no words."

– Pope Francis

"My father made it through thanks to his faith. He frequently went to Mass, prayed the Rosary, and even had a kneeler in his room where he prayed alone to Jesus."

– Gabriela Vieto

Jorge's Example

When my father was 54 years old, he was diagnosed with Sarcoïdosis, a rare inflammatory disease that can affect any organ in the body. Due to his condition, my father had to endure frequent fevers and pains throughout his body and live in great uncertainty.

However, he decided not to get carried away by the pain and did his best to continue his daily activities. He had his own company; he was passionate about his work. He liked to talk with the employees.

Two years before dying, he wrote a letter to his grandchildren in which he gave them instructions for life. The message was to be delivered when the grandchildren turned 15 years old. His faith supported his life. He frequently went to Mass, prayed the Rosary, and even had a kneeler in his room where he prayed alone to Jesus and with us, his children.

Dad was always a man who enjoyed many hobbies. He enjoyed playing the organ, taking his remote control boats to a lake, playing the accordion, and dancing with his loving wife, my mom, Norma.

After suffering from Sarcoïdosis for 19 years, doctors diagnosed him with acute leukemia. In his last year of life, he took some trips to spend time with the family.

A month and a half before he passed away, my father wrote a letter which was read at his funeral. In it, he expressed all his love to the whole family and left instructions for his most loved ones to follow.

On February 17, 2018, he requested a Mass at his home and invited all those he loved most to say goodbye to each of us. My dad passed away the next day.

Gabriela Vieto, Jorge's daughter

How can you follow Jorge's example?

You can talk to God or pray the Rosary.

Listen to Mass or a spiritual service in person or virtually.

Write letters or express your love to your loved ones.

"We all have some physical, mental or spiritual paralysis and only by knowing the love of the Father we can overcome everything and get out of those cages that trap us. Thank you Paula for reminding us that we must always trust in Jesus!"

– Dr. Gerry Sotomayor

Be confident that your illness is a vehicle for evangelization, and you will find your mission.

— Paula Umana

The Ramp of Joy

My story with Pipo began when a friend invited me to her house for the first time. When I got there, I was stunned to find a ramp in the home. It surprised me because it is unusual for a person like me with a wheelchair to find a ramp in an ordinary house.

I asked my friend about the ramp, and she replied that it was for her father-in-law, a Cuban man called Pipo, who lived on the second floor and was very ill. I told my friend that I would like to meet him. When I entered his room, Pipo was confused to see a young woman in a wheelchair in front of him.

My new friend was very reserved initially, so I began to sing Cuban songs of yesteryear that reminded him of his childhood. I fell in love with him. Pipo listened to me carefully when I spoke to him about God. During my subsequent visits, he talked and smiled, and his nurse loved that. She saw an improvement in her patient's health and mood.

I realized that when I arrived at the house, Pipo was sad, and at the end of the visit, he radiated happiness and his heart was full of joy.

Paula Umana

Be alert

Learn to recognize the spiritual needs of the people around you so you can touch their hearts.

"Jesus, forgive my sins. Come into my heart. I want you to be my Lord and my savior."

Amen.

The Ramp that Takes us to Heaven

My friend Pipo's life gradually faded away. One day, when he was very sick and I was going to his house to visit him, my body began to shake because I had to tell him about God and death.

With much love, I told him, "Pipo, you are going to die. Do you want to prepare your heart for God? Do you want to ask forgiveness for your sins?" He nodded and said yes. We made a beautiful prayer in which he gave his heart to the Lord. He also accepted a priest's visit to put the holy oils on him and give him Communion.

A few days later, I woke up in the early morning, and because I couldn't sleep again, I started to pray. At six in the morning, I received a text message from Pipo's family informing me that he had died a couple of hours earlier. He passed away six months after our first meeting.

The most important thing for a sick person is to know for sure what his destiny will be when he is no longer among his loved ones.

If you are sick, know that Jesus has cleared the way for you to put your faith in Him. Be confident that one day you will be in His presence.

Paula Umana

Talk about death:

We know that we are all going to die. Talk to your loved ones straightforwardly about death, put your personal life in order, ask for forgiveness, and forgive. Prepare yourself spiritually for eternal life.

Prayer

Jesus, forgive my sins. Come into my heart. I want you to be my Lord and my savior.

Amen.

Resource

The sacrament of the anointing of the sick has great power to bring relief and salvation.

Four Words

Months before a revelation, I couldn't feel God with me. I felt He was silent, and that silence made me have the sensation of being a dried-up tree, unable to bear fruit.

In March 2015, at the break of dawn, I was in a hospital bed awaiting a diagnosis when four words reached my heart: "I am your certainty." At that time, I had no idea how important these words would be, yet they would sustain me spiritually for the next few days.

Doctors diagnosed me with inoperable pancreatic cancer with metastasis to the lungs. They told me I had three to six months to live. The news shocked my entire family and me as well.

We can catch a glimpse of two points of view: the human and the divine. I remembered the message: "I am your certainty." Certain of what? I wondered. Soon after, I discovered the assurance of God's love, of His care, of His company, that our lives are in His hands.

Those four precious words were my support in the darkest moments of my life when pain and sadness wanted to take charge of my faith. Every beat of my heart brings to mind those four wise words: "I am your certainty."

Ana Polini

Ana passed away on March 7, 2017.

Repeat this prayer

Jesus, you are my certainty. I trust you. I will find courage and strength to go through the suffering. Thank you, God, that you have made me part of your kingdom through Jesus. Amen.

> "I am your certitude." Certitude of what? I later understood that it was about a certitude of love, of care, of being prepared, of feeling the presence of a God who has our fate in His hands.

– Ana Polini

¿What would God paint?

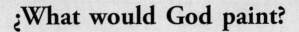When we abandon our fears to God and
His will, we receive peace and courage
to endure whatever comes our way.

– Sally

A White Canvas

A chapter in my chronic health story has to do with the loss of teeth in my lower jaw due to a bone infection. My goal was to be infection-free, ready for a removable denture, and finally have dental implant surgery.

After many delays, the day of the appointment with the periodontist arrived to start the treatment. Unfortunately, the X-rays gave the doctor the indication that another type of surgery and many healing months were necessary before the planned process. My disappointment was huge.

That same day, I visited the endocrinologist, who noticed that emotionally I was not well, and I told him the reason for my sadness and despair.

The endocrinologist, who had also gone through similar sufferings, advised me to remember some biblical characters from the Psalms, who, beyond what they thought, always ended up praising God.

A second medical opinion brought my soul back to my body as he told me that no further operation was necessary, and my dental implant surgery was successful.

When we abandon our fears to God and His will, we receive peace and courage to endure whatever comes our way.

Sally

Read this prayer out loud

Lord, I offer myself to you as a blank canvas. I'm not going to worry about what You choose to paint. Teach me at all times to accept your brushstrokes. Amen

"What are you going to do, Mom? Are you going to stay in that bed crying? You need to live your life. Live it with what you have available in your body if it is a leg or just an arm. Live your life with what you have available and move on."

– Marie Sautré

Don't Feel Sorry for Yourself

I was on my way home from a medical appointment at the Vanderbilt Neuromuscular Disorders Clinic in Tennessee. A doctor assured me that I would not be able to walk again. His words left me heartbroken and filled with despair.

I thought about my family and raising my children. I would not walk with them hand in hand. I would have to say goodbye to the active life I used to have, my tennis students, and the tournaments I organized. I felt overwhelmed. I needed to cry, to vent my feelings to someone.

I did not choose my husband nor my sister nor a friend. I decided to talk to my 15-year-old daughter. Marie came into my room, and I started crying. "Marie," I told her, "the doctor says I'll never walk, he doesn't see any progress in me."

My teenage daughter looked at me and said a phrase that I will never forget: "What are you going to do, Mom? Are you going to stay in that bed crying? You need to live your life. Live it with what you have available in your body if it is a leg or just an arm. Live your life with what you have available and move on."

When I heard those words, my soul filled with courage, and I decided to open my tennis academy despite a physical disability.

Paula Umana

Application

No matter how many blows life gives you, don't feel sorry for yourself. Fill yourself with courage and move on.

Make a list of all the good things you have in your life and all the things you can do with what you have.

> "Ten years after the accident, I dare to say that God had a plan for my life today. Now I live happily free."

— Natalia Vindas

Life is Like the Waves

I am paraplegic due to a traffic accident. Now I use a wheelchair to get around. After a tough time adapting to my reality, I discovered, thanks to a friend, a great joy in my life: surfing.

My purpose has become advocating for the rights of people with disabilities, and I became one of the world's best competitors in adapted surfing. I found a way to give happiness back to people with disabilities by teaching them to enjoy nature. I have worked to transform tourist destinations into accessible vacation sites for anyone and everyone.

Ten years after the accident, I dare to say that God had a plan for my life today. Now I live happily free.

Life is like the waves of the ocean. When I'm surfing, every time a wave comes, I have to go out of my way to move from the foam to the surf line. Sometimes I make bad decisions, like when I take a wrong wave, and I can end up wallowing. However, when I catch the right wave, I feel free and fulfilled.

Life is like waves; when we make wrong decisions, difficult trials can come, but when we manage to take the right wave, we will feel freedom and joy. Don't forget that you don't have to do everything correctly, or your life won't flow smoothly. Life is continuous learning. Sometimes the ocean waves will knock you down; other times, you will know that you took the right wave.

Natalia Vindas, Bronze Medal, Adapted Surfing World Cup 2017

Exercise

Like the ocean, life is variable and full of challenges. Learn to adapt by taking one wave at a time and enjoy it.

"Optimism is the belief that leads to success. Nothing can be done without hope and trust."

Helen Keller

"Cling to hope, let yourself be surprised by God and live with joy."

— Pope Francis

"Today I am a free, strong, brave woman, and I know who I am. My being is filled with God. I have peace and fulfillment."

– Maureen Valverde

Let Nothing Disturb You

Isuffered sexual abuse and emotional and spiritual assaults by a close family member for 25 years. That terrible experience left me with scars such as panic attacks, anxiety disorder, depression, night terror, addictions, fear for my life, and suicide attempts.

I received psychological and psychiatric treatments. Doctors prescribed all kinds of medications. My parents knew nothing of my previous abuse. In their desperation to improve my health, they spoke with a priest who recommended the Peniel Method, a psychospiritual transformation system that manages to heal all areas of life with the help of the Holy Spirit.

Seeing my parents so distressed and watching some testimonial videos, I decided to give it a try, although I didn't have much faith. To my surprise, I felt better mentally and spiritually after just two months of meetings with a facilitator.

Today I am a free, strong, brave woman, and I know who I am. My being is filled with God. I have peace and fulfillment.

Maureen Valverde

If this story resonated with you, and you'd like more information, visit the PENIEL Method account on Facebook: @MetodoPENIEL

Memorize

Let nothing disturb you

Let nothing disturb you,

let nothing frighten you,

everything passes,

God does not move;

peace comes to nothing,

whoever has nothing and lacks everything,

but has God, lacks nothing;

only God is enough.

— Saint Teresa of Avila

> *Close your door on yourself and call on your beloved Jesus; stay with Him in your room, you will not find so much peace in another place.*

– Tomás of Kempis

"I changed, and now I give myself to God from the moment I open my eyes until I close them. I found security in Jesus Christ and the Word of God."

– Corey Wavle

From Addiction to Conversion

At age eighteen, doctors diagnosed me with type 1 diabetes, and the doctors could not tell me the origin of the disease. The test results came at a challenging time in my life due to being addicted to pornography and drugs and suffering from depression. I lived angry at the world, my family, myself, and God.

I became emotionally, physically, and spiritually unstable. I cut myself off from people who cared about me, but God did not abandon me. I realized deep down that there was still hope.

Four years after my diagnosis, I stopped ignoring my diabetes and began to face my fears. I changed, and now I give myself to God from the moment I open my eyes until I close them. I found security in Jesus Christ and the Word of God.

I discovered a therapeutic interpersonal connection, a link with God the Father, with my peers and with my family through self-love.

Corey Wavle, a child of God

Keys to overcoming addictions

1. I am weak. My life is unmanageable without God.
2. Only God can heal me.
3. I put my will and my life in the hands of God.
4. I take a moral inventory of myself without fear.
5. I acknowledge my mistakes before God and others.

6. I am willing for God to remove all my character flaws.

7. I humbly ask God to free me from my shortcomings.

8. I make a list of the people I have offended, and I make amends for my faults.

9. I will make amends with others except when doing so hurts them.

10. I will do a personal inventory, and when I'm wrong, I accept it.

11. I am with God through prayer. I ask to know God's will and have the strength to carry it out.

12. I will bring this message to addicts who have had a spiritual awakening.

PART FOUR

The Power of the Blood of Christ

I felt awful for several days. I had a high temperature, weakness, and a headache. I was baffled and didn't know what was wrong with me. I got up to go to the bathroom, and while I was sitting on the toilet, I called Marina, a young woman who helps me around the house. I told her I didn't know what I had, but I felt terrible. Marina tells me that my eyes rolled back after I said those words; my jaw dropped to the left side, and I passed out.

When I woke up, I felt a wonderful sense of peace and love. Marina held me in her arms and cried out to Jesus with all her might. She told me that she took me in her arms and smeared oil on my forehead when I passed out. Confused and afraid that she would never see me conscious again, she began to scream with all her might. "The blood of Christ has power, Jesus is the doctor par excellence. The blood of Christ has power, Jesus is the doctor par excellence."

I will never forget the peace-loving feeling I felt when I woke up from that loss of consciousness. I told Marina that I had enjoyed passing out because of the love I felt Christ had given me.

Paula Umana

> *Is anyone among you sick? He should summon the presbyters of the church, and they should pray over him and anoint [him] with oil in the name of the Lord, and the prayer of faith will save the sick person, and the Lord will raise him up. If he has committed any sins, he will be forgiven.*
>
> **– James 5: 14-15**

Action

When you feel sick and don't know what to do, even if you don't have any strength or motivation, cry out to God with all your heart and say, "The blood of Christ has power, Jesus is the doctor by excellence."

"*Is anyone among you sick? He should summon the presbyters of the church, and they should pray over him and anoint [him] with oil in the name of the Lord, and the prayer of faith will save the sick person, and the Lord.*"

– James 5:14

Saint Joseph Protects You

I was preparing to be ordained a Catholic priest when all of a sudden, I began to have excruciating headaches that led to migraines. Every time I felt symptoms, the fear started, and I tried to do everything possible to avoid the pain.

I was like this until learning that the best thing I could do for myself was accept the onset of symptoms and withdraw from activities. I had to go to my room and rest. Accepting the migraine with ease helped me feel better, much faster.

Years later, as a priest, I began to pray a novena to Saint Joseph to ask for my health. I was praying the novena when I felt such intense pain that I ended up in the emergency room where I was diagnosed with gallbladder stones and quite advanced diabetes.

I felt Saint Joseph had protected me because the visit to the hospital for the gallbladder helped me realize that I had to watch my health and diet. I am not a friend of needles and did not want to use insulin in the future.

The experience helped me realize that the father of Jesus helps us in the face of any difficulty; he is the saint par excellence after the Virgin Mary, and he is willing to assist us in whatever we need.

Catholic Priest Anonymous Atlanta, United States

Who is Saint Joseph?

When pain comes, accept it calmly and ask Saint Joseph to help you.

We care about physical health, but the priority must be spiritual health.

" *We care about physical health, but the priority must be spiritual health.* "

– **Virginia Umaña**

"Even though I walk through the valley of the shadow of death, I will fear no evil, for you are with me;your rod and your staff comfort me."

Psalm 23: 4

Your Word Sustains Me

A few years ago, an autoimmune disease known as Superficial Pemphigus attacked my body, causing blisters and sores on the skin.

The disease caused uncontrollable itching, as well as breakouts, swelling, and cracks on my skin. For more than three months, I suffered irritation all over my body that kept me from sleeping. My skin was full of lesions so that even the cotton sheet caused me pain. These were challenging moments in my life.

To cope with so many nights of torture, I repeated three biblical verses that I kept in my mind and heart. Thank God, today, I am ninety percent recovered from the disease.

Georgina Umaña, Christian leader

Words of Life

The verses below were my most incredible resource for enduring pain and anguish:

1. *Even though I walk through the valley of the shadow of death, I will fear no evil, for you are with me; your rod and your staff comfort me.*

   Psalm 23: 4

2. *Because you have the Lord for your refuge and have made the Most High your stronghold, No evil shall befall you, no affliction come near your tent.*

   Psalm 91: 9-10

3.   *Consider it all joy, my brothers, when you encounter various trials, for you know that the testing of your faith produces perseverance. And let perseverance be perfect, so that you may be perfect and complete, lacking in nothing.*

James 1: 2-4

Application

Use the bible verses above during times of pain and suffering.

Although the world is full of suffering, it is also full of overcoming.

– Helen Keller

After the Storm

A group of women invited me to give a lecture, and the topic of the meeting was to talk about "Hope in the midst of suffering." It was a memorable night when I took the stage. I felt empowered, and I had mastered the subject. The talk was based on handling suffering during illness.

Five years had passed from the time when I became quadriplegic until I could walk again. I was convinced that I was the person who knew the most about how to manage suffering in illness. Furthermore, I had written a book about it.

Four days after the conference, I became very ill and ended up in the hospital emergency room. They told me I had pneumonia, and I was immediately isolated. I was there three days, and during that time, I could not pronounce the word Jesus.

I couldn't accept that I was weak again and I didn't know how to ask for Jesus's help; I just couldn't bring myself to do it. I felt terrible, incapable, and vulnerable. It was impossible to lift my eyes to heaven and say a prayer. Inconceivable to receive advice from a family member or friend.

When I returned home, I understood that I am a vulnerable human being, full of mistakes and that there are days when I cannot raise my eyes to heaven or speak to God because I feel weak.

If you have those days when you feel desperate, abandoned, unwilling to receive advice, support, or prayer, don't be distressed. We are human beings; after the storm, peace will come.

Paula Umana

He said to them, "Why are you terrified, O you of little faith?" Then he got up, rebuked the winds and the sea, and there was great calm.

– Matthew 8:26

Prayer

Thank you, Lord, because peace always comes after the storm.

> *He said to them, "Why are you terrified, O you of little faith?" Then he got up, rebuked the winds and the sea, and there was great calm.*
>
> **– Matthew 8:26**

"I live for Christ. I am no longer in control of what will happen each day with my daughter. What I do know is that I surrender myself to the Lord entirely."

— Beth Borés, María's mother

I Live for Christ

When my daughter Maria was twelve years old, I received a phone call from her school informing me that the school had transferred her to a psychiatric hospital due to an emergency. When I got to school, they told me that my daughter had self-mutilation marks on her arms. Ever since then, my family has lived through years of suffering.

Maria has tried to kill herself several times; her body is full of scars from the damage done during the traumatic experiences of her childhood and adolescence. In these eight years, Maria has been admitted several times to psychiatric hospitals.

Despite going through this situation and being the mother of seven children, in 2014, I went on a spiritual retreat that transformed my life and taught me to deal with suffering.

I learned to no longer live for my desires, my worries, or my pain. I live for Christ. I am no longer in control of what will happen each day with my daughter. What I do know is that I surrender myself to the Lord entirely.

I learned to pray and not ask for what I wanted. I began to focus on an immense and powerful God. Worshiping Him is among the things I enjoy the most. When I play worship and praise music, I raise my arms and lose myself in my habitual routine.

Today with a diagnosis of Limited Personality Disorder, Maria tries a new treatment. She is at home, and I dedicate myself one hundred percent to her care with all my heart and love.

Beth, Barcelona, Spain

A spiritual retreat will change your life.

Exercise

Use music as a means to help you cope with your suffering. Praising God lets you know that He is sovereign and worshipping Him takes your focus off of yourself.

> *I learned to worship an immense and powerful God and not to ask for what I wanted.*
>
> – Beth Borés, María's mother

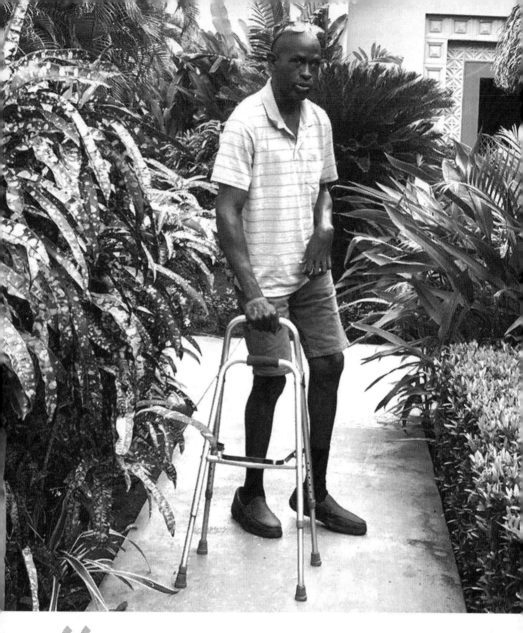

"I have a Bible open on my bed that I read day and night, and although at first it was difficult to understand, the Holy Spirit helped me understand it. I found all the comfort and peace I need there."

– Lloyd Hickinson

Lloyd's Treasure

I was born with a disease known as Sickle Cell, a genetic condition for red blood cells. During my childhood and adolescence, I spent half the time in the hospital, where they administered morphine to alleviate the disease's pain.

My mother, Angelica, always told me: "You are a child of God; you are a child of God." One afternoon, when I was 19 years old, I visited a Texas shopping mall, and I saw that several people gathered in a circle praying. I approached with curiosity, they talked to me about Jesus, and they invited me to their church. That's how I met my Savior.

At the age of fifty-three, I suffered a stroke, and since then, I have half of my body damaged. Today I live alone in an apartment in Aruba. I have many physical limitations that often cause me frustration and loneliness; however, Jesus fills me with patience and courage. My greatest treasure is having found the word of God.

I have a Bible open on my bed that I read day and night, and although at first it was difficult to understand, the Holy Spirit helped me understand it. I found all the comfort and peace I need there.

One of my favorite verses is Jeremiah 29: 13, which says: *"When you look for me, you will find me. Yes, when you seek me with all your heart."*

Lloyd

The treasure

In a book or an audio format, the Bible is the best resource you can use to comfort your soul. The word of God is alive and powerful.

> **Children are the engine that motivates us beyond our own strength.**
>
> — Liliana García Barkes

Clarita danced for me

I arrived at a hospital emergency room after several days with a fever and fainting at home. After rigorous tests and a CT scan, I was diagnosed with pneumonia, and I ended up hospitalized. I felt ill; I had a fever and body aches, but what made me feel desperate was being confined to a room.

Although weeks later, I acquired the knowledge of being infected with COVID 19, my confinement caused me such despair that I could not pray and had no inner peace.

Amid my anguish, I received a short video on my cell phone in which my daughter Clara danced while washing her hands and made light of my illness. For a few seconds, I forgot all my afflictions and laughed out loud as I watched two short videos with a comical song and choreography.

My young children Charles, Felicitée, and Ana Cecilia contacted me via video call to tell me that they loved and missed me.

My children's love and care were the best medicine in these moments of pain and suffering. Children are the engine that motivates us beyond our strength.

Paula Umana

Virtual love resources

Use video calls, applications on your cell phone, and any technological aid to maintain communication with your loved ones. Love will help you manage pain and suffering.

Sing when you bathe and dance in front of the mirror!

“We can achieve everything we set out to do. Each of us knows our own strength to succeed in life.”

– Juan Maggi

Conquer your Himalayas

When I was one year old, I was diagnosed with Polio, a viral disease that causes muscle weakness and paralysis and affects motor skills.

My childhood was full of challenges but also abundant in love and fun. As I reached adolescence, my demeanor changed, and I came to hate my body and my disability. I ate junk food, smoked, and drank alcohol until one day, when I was 37 years old, I had a heart attack. I realized that life had sent me a warning sign.

I decided to completely reinvent myself and put all of my energy and faith into becoming a high-performance handbike athlete. With a lot of effort, patience, and tons of equipment, I fulfilled two of my biggest dreams: participating in the New York City Marathon and reaching the top of the Himalayas on a hand bike.

I recommend you don't put your eyes on the medical diagnosis and focus on the prognosis that arises from you. We can achieve everything we set out to do. Each of us knows our own strength to succeed in life.

Juan Maggi, Cordoba, Argentina

Daily challenge

What is important and decisive in life is not what happens to us, but the attitude we take toward what happens.

What is your challenge today?

Never limit yourself!

Jesús en Ti Confío

> *For the sake of His sorrowful Passion, have mercy on us and on the whole world.*

The Prayer to Divine Mercy

I was 36 years old when I first heard the prayer to Divine Mercy, the prayers for the healing and conversion of the spirit of the sick and dying revealed to the Polish nun Faustina Kowalska in 1935.

One can say the prayer at different times of the day, but it is recommended to do it at three in the afternoon, "the hour of mercy" when Jesus died. The Feast of Divine Mercy is celebrated on the second Sunday of Easter.

Fifteen years ago, my life was full of anguish and without peace due to my husband's alcoholism and assaults.

On one of the days that Hugo disappeared because he went out for drinks, I turned on the television and stopped on a Catholic channel transmitting prayers. My daughter, Ariana, who was four years old, started repeating the song of worship.

The next three days, at three in the afternoon, I tuned in to the channel to hear the prayers. On Friday of that week, I went to a church to pray before the Blessed Sacrament, and a friend gave me a picture of Divine Mercy. I prayed very fervently and asked the Lord to help my husband. Hugo stopped drinking and recently completed fourteen years of sobriety.

My husband and I consider ourselves worshipers of the Blessed Sacrament of the Altar of Divine Mercy. I also dedicate myself to visiting the sick and dying so that with prayer, they may find the peace of God.

Evelyn Castro, servant dedicated
to spreading Divine Mercy

Application

Find more information about the prayer to Divine Mercy. You can pray it for yourself and for others. It is beneficial and powerful.

"I also dedicate myself to visiting the sick and dying so that with prayer of the Divine Mercy, they may find the peace of God.»

— Evelyn Castro

> **"** By the sweat of your face shall you get bread to eat, until you return to the ground, from which you were taken; For you are dirt, and to dirt you shall return. **"**

– Genesis 3:19

My Visit Through the Threshold

Sports are and have been a constant activity in my life. I grew up playing in Turrialba's town square, in Costa Rica, and swimming in the Torres River.

At age thirty, I became a tennis player. With more than forty years and seven children, I figured out that if I did not take care of myself, I would not have the temperament, the strength, or the tolerance to raise and support a large family.

I became interested in biking and bought a motorcycle. When I was 68 years old, I decided to embark on an adventure on wheels in Central America. I joined a group of motorcyclists that left Costa Rica and reached Guatemala.

On the way back, I suffered a severe accident in Honduras that caused detachment of the mesenteric veins and fractures of the ribs, pelvis, and arm. During surgery, my blood pressure dropped to zero for five minutes, but my heart kept beating.

During the operation, I had an out-of-body experience. I felt myself leaving my body and entering the threshold of death. I saw myself as a spectator of my procedure. The nurse said, "We are losing him!" I laughed and said to myself, "My time has not come yet."

With the light at the end of the tunnel, I could see my mother, Lucrecia, from a distance, and an indescribable peace entered me, sheer bliss where time and space did not exist.

I understood that death is beautiful. I lost the fear and that feeling of uncertainty. The self-preservation instinct in us is powerful, but death is a transition between different planes. I think we shouldn't worry because it is a beautiful feeling.

At ninety years old and after overcoming a gallbladder operation, a heart attack, and cancer in one eye, I enjoy the company of my wife, Virginia, my grandchildren, and my great-grandchildren. And every Tuesday and Thursday, I play tennis with my dear friends.

— *Dr. Carlos Umaña Gil, dentist, Paula's Father.*

Don't be afraid of death

We know by our faith that the final departure is nothing more than a change of residence.

Visualize the journey that one day will take you to eternal life.

If your physical strength allows it, integrate exercise into your life, as it will bring you both physical and spiritual benefits.

By the sweat of your face shall you get bread to eat, Until you return to the ground, from which you were taken; For you are dirt, and to dirt you shall return.

— **Genesis 3:19**

Start by doing what's necessary; then do what's possible; and suddenly you are doing the impossible.

– Saint Francis of Assisi

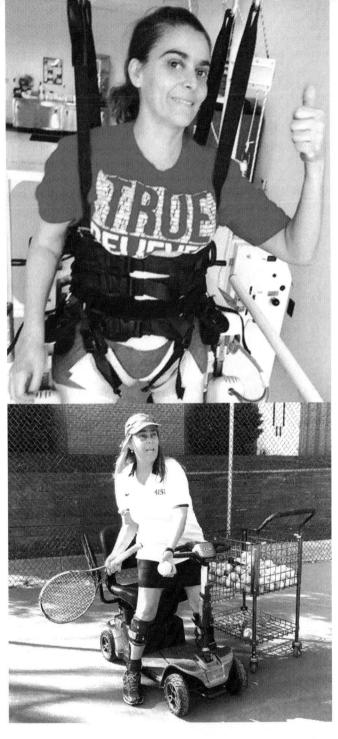

" Where there's a will there's a way "

There is Always a Way

Diagnosis: Muscular atrophy in the hands, legal blindness that would prevent me from driving a car, and paraplegia. Medical ruling: Using a wheelchair, not having independence, and not working as a tennis instructor.

Despite adversity, life taught me that there are ways to find a solution to any challenge that comes our way when we have a disability.

When I needed to move from the wheelchair to the bed, I used a board to slide from one place to another. To walk, by a miracle of God, I got special devices that allow me to do it with limitations, but that gives me freedom.

I learned to dance strapped by a belt to the stair baluster so as not to fall. I have some bongos that I play with my hands, and I have fun with the sound of music, and that makes me very happy.

I had to relearn how to operate a vehicle by putting on bioptic glasses and using manual driving controls. I have a motorized tricycle to give my tennis lessons.

I started giving motivational lectures and writing. These activities allow me to share my experiences to encourage others who are suffering. These changes resulted from many years of effort and overcoming the fear of doing something new.

Since I was little, I learned from my parents to be brave. I follow Carlos's example, who still enjoys playing tennis at ninety. Virginia, who always found a way to get ahead with her seven children, still inspires me. My achievements have been thanks to the therapists' support and the financial help of friends and family. I am also deeply grateful to organizations such as the Order of Malta that made my pilgrimage to the Shrine of Our Lady of Lourdes in France possible.

When illness or affliction affects us, we tend to fill ourselves with physical, spiritual, and emotional limitations. Fear invades us because we think that things will not be as they were before.

After my experience, I can say that there will always be a way to cope with or overcome our health and life challenges. Don't let anything or anyone steal your dreams.

Where there is a will, everything is possible with God!

Paula Umana

There is always a way

If you feel sadness, disappointment, or frustration about things that you can no longer do, ask the Holy Spirit to give you creativity to find alternatives, allowing you to have the freedom to feel good about yourself.

With your friends and family's help, search for the financial assistance needed to facilitate the physical changes required for your current lifestyle.

References

American Cancer Society. (September 8th 2019). [Internet]. Treatment of Ductal Carcinoma in Situ (DCIS). United States. [visited on February 19th 2021]. Obtained from:https://www.cancer.org/cancer/breast-cancer/treatment/treatment-of-breast-cancer-by-stage/treatment-of-ductal-carcinoma-in-situ-dcis.html

Our Lady of Los Angeles Basilica. [Internet]. Cartago, Costa Rica. [visited on December 2020]. Obtained from: https://www.santuarionacional.org/

Carratalá,F. (January- February 2015). The poetic work of Teresa de Ávila. Notes from Language and Literature on the V Centenary of the birth of Santa Teresa, Madrid. [consulted on February 9th 2021]. Obtained from: https://www.cdlmadrid.org/wp-content/uploads/2016/02/apuntes-lengua-0115.pdf

Centers for the Disease Control and Prevention. [Internet]. Department of Health and Human Services of the United States. Obtained from: https://www.cdc.gov/spanish/index.html

Fernández Piera, Juan María. Kempis of a Sick Person: Brief guide to live the disease.

Ediciones Sígueme. Salamanca, Spain 2007.

Christopher & Dana Reeve Foundation. [Internet]. International services in Spanish. United States. Obtained from: https://www.christopherreeve.org

Multiple Sclerosis Foundation. Multiple Sclerosis Observatory. (June 21st 2019). [Internet].¿Which are the symptoms for multiple sclerosis? Revised by: Patricia Mulero. Col·legide Metges de Catalunya (collegiate number 51.938). Barcelona, España. [consulted on February 8th 2021]. Obtained from:

https://www.observatorioesclerosismultiple.com/es/la-esclerosis-multiple/cuales-son-los-sintomas/cuales-son-los-sintomas-de-la-esclerosis-multiple/

Multiple Sclerosis Foundation. Multiple Sclerosis Observatory. (May 11th 2020). [Internet].

Depression in people with multiple sclerosis. Barcelona, Spain. [consulted on February 8th 2021]. Obtained from:

https://www.observatorioesclerosismultiple.com/es/vivir/aspectos-psicologicos/la-depresion-en-personas-con-esclerosis-multiple/

In-pacient.es. (May 28th 2015). [Internet]. Speech disorders perceived by MS patient do not always correspond to the specialist assessment. Spain. [consulted on February 8th 2021]. Obtained from:

https://www.in-pacient.es/noticia/los-trastornos-del-habla-percibidos-por-el-paciente-de-em-no-siempre-se-corresponde-con-la-valoracion-del-especialista/

National Health Institutes. [Internet]. Bethesda (MD). United States. Obtained from:

https://salud.nih.gov/

National Eye Institute. [Internet]. Bethesda (MD). National Health Institutes. United States. (July 10th 2019)Low vision. [consulted on February 9th 2021]. Obtained from: https://www.nei.nih.gov/learn-about-eye-health/en-espanol/la-baja-vision Keller,Helen. Optimism. An Essay.Published on November 1903.

D.B. Updike,The Merrympount Press, Boston. Project Gutenberg. Publication date: March 13th 2010. [EBook #31622] [consulted on February 28th 2021].Obtained from: http://www.gutenberg.org/files/31622/31622-0.txt

The Bible USCCB https://bible.usccb.org/bible

Lupus Research Alliance. [Internet]. About Lupus. United States. Obtained from: https://www.lupusresearch.org/en espanol/acerca-del-lupus/

Mayo Clinic. [Internet]. International services in Spanish. United States. Obtained from: https://www.mayoclinic.org/es-es

MedlinePlus® in Spanish. [Internet]. Health information for you. Bethesda (MD): National Medical Library of the United States. National Health Institutes. Obtained from:

https://medlineplus.gov/spanish/

PENIEL Method. [Facebook]. Costa Rica. Obtained from: https://www.facebook.com/MetodoPENIEL/

National Breast Cancer Foundation, Inc. (Medically Reviewed on April 15, 2020). [Internet].About Breast Cancer. What Types of Cancer Are Diagnosed As Stage 0 and 1 Breast Cancer? [consulted on February 19th 2021]. Obtained from: https://www.nationalbreastcancer.org/breast-cancer-stage-0-and-stage-1

Pope Francis. General Audience. Wednesday, January 4th 2017. ©

Librería Editrice Vaticana. [consulted on February 26th 2021]. Obtained from: http://www.vatican.va/content/francesco/es/audiences/2017/documents/papa-francesco_20170104_udienza-generale.html

Pope Francis.Homily of the Holy Father Francis.Wednesday, July 24th 2013. Holy Mass in the Basilica of the Sanctuary of Our Lady of Aparecida. Apostolic Journey to Rio de Janeiro on the occasion of the XXVIII World Youth Day. © Librería Editrice Vaticana. [consulted on February 26th 2021]. Obtained from:

http://www.vatican.va/content/francesco/es/homilies/2013/
documents/papa-francesco_20130724_gmg-omelia-aparecida.
html

Royal Spanish Academy. (2005). [Internet]. Digital Library.
In Pan-Hispanic Dictionary of Doubts. Obtained from: https://
www.rae.es/dpd/

Rowan, C. (June 2002). [Internet]. Multiple Sclerosis.
Hope in the Research. National Institute of Neurological
Disorders and Vascular Accidents. National Health Institutes.
NIH Publication Number: 02-75. United States. [consulted on
February 8th 2021].

Obtained from: https://espanol.ninds.nih.gov/trastornos/
span_esclerosis.pdf

Rudolph, Wilma. n.p. n.d n.pag. The Golden Quotes.
Public Domain. Obtained from: https://www.thegoldenquotes.
net/achievement-quotes/

Saint Francis of Assisi. Start doing what is necessary,
then what is possible, and suddenly you will be doing the
impossible.

By: P. Dennis Doren L.C. Source: Catholic.net Published
on Catholic.net. [consulted on February 28th 2021]. Obtained
from:https://es.catholic.net/op/articulos/47417/cat/305/
comienza-haciendo-lo-que-es-necesario-despues-lo-posible-y-
de-repente-estaras-haciendo-lo-imposible.html#modal

Saint Pio of Pietrelcina. How to keep giving glory to
God when everything in my life goes wrong? By: Solange
Paredes. Source: Catholic-link.com. Published on: Catholic.net.
[consulted on February 28th 2021]. Obtained from: https://
es.catholic.net/op/articulos/71578/como-seguir-dando-gloria-
a-dios-cuando-todo-en-mi-vida-sale-mal#modal

Santuario de Nuestra Señora de Lourdes. Francia. [Internet]. Obtenido de: https://www.lourdes-france.org/es/

Shepherd Center. [Internet]. Atlanta, Georgia, United States. Obtained from: https://www.shepherd.org/

American Society Against Cancer. [Internet]. United States. Obtained from: https://www.cancer.org/es.html

Surfemotion.

(September 28th 2015). [Internet]. How to get your first wave. [Blog Article].

[consulted on February 5th 2021]. Obtained from:

https://surfmocion.com/2015/09/28/como-pillar-tu-primera-ola/

Tennis on wheels. [Facebook]. Costa Rica.

Obtained from: https://www.facebook.com/TenisSobreRuedasCR

Vanderbilt Neuromuscular Disorders Clinic. [Internet]. Nashville, Tennessee, United States.

Obtained from: https://www.vanderbilthealth.com/program/neuromuscular-disorders

❝The stories that Paula has collected, together with her own story, are an eloquent expression of faith and hope in the midst of the most difficult circumstances that illness and suffering could bring to any of us. Instead of being defeated with a victim mentality, each one found new courage and determination in God by abandoning himself or herself to his love and Providence. In doing so they transformed their lives and are witnesses of the power of supernatural hope. I have had the privilege of knowing Paula for years and I am always edified by the joy with which she has built a new life after overcoming so many challenges. This book is a tribute to God and to the transformative power of his love. **❞**

– Fr. Lino Otero LC
Regnum Christi Local Director
Atlanta, GA

❝ Many years ago I heard a Bible study instructor say that "all sunshine makes a desert." In other words, if we look back on our lives, we realize that it's those struggles, as severe as some may be, when offered up to God, that help us to become fertile soil ready to bare wonderful fruit. Paula's collection of real life stories in 40 Gifts of Hope provides the perfect spiritual forecast, so to speak. The book exemplifies in great and very personal detail, how the Lord's love can break through, if we let it, even the darkest of storm clouds, making way for a brighter and more meaningful future. ❞

– Teresa Tomeo
Media Expert, Motivational Speaker,
Best Selling Author

"Seeking hope and joy in the midst of trials and suffering of our life."

– Father Tamiru Atraga
Holy Spirit Catholic Church, Atlanta

"We all need stories like Paula's to remind us of a greater hope. Through these short stories and lessons, we have a guide map to suffer strong."

– Katherine Wolf
Hope Heals

"Do not be afraid of pain, let the Holy Spirit do his work in you."

– Mother Andrea de Jesus

"We all have some physical, mental or spiritual paralysis and only by knowing the love of the Father can we overcome everything and get out of those cages that trap us. Thank you Paula for reminding us that we must always trust in Jesus!"

– Dr. Gerry Sotomayor
Gynecologist

Paula Umana (San José, Costa Rica, 1974) is an author, motivational speaker, and businesswoman who graduated in International Trade from the Universidad International de las Americas in San Jose, Costa Rica. She completed the Dynamic Public Speaking program from the University of Washington in Seattle. She speaks Spanish, English, and French.

In the 1990's she was the number one tennis player in her country and in Central America; she was featured in the world ranking of the Women's Tennis Association. Her experience in the sport brought her to establish *Coach Paula Tennis*, an academy for children and young adults in Atlanta, Georgia, United States.

After giving birth to her fifth child in 2015, Paula fell ill due to a neurological disorder known as Chronic Inflammatory Demyelinating Polyneuropathy. She became quadriplegic. Her certainty in her faith helped support her during the intense physiotherapies and helped her endure difficult moments. Now she walks with the help of orthopedic devices for her legs.

In 2020 she received the MundoHispánico award in the sports category. She also participated in the forum Breaking Paradigms in Sports, from The Women Economic Forum Costa Rica. She is a part of the Catholic Speakers Organization and participates in forums and seminars.

Paula belongs to the parishes of Holy Spirit Catholic Church and St. Francis de Sales Catholic Church in the state of Georgia.

Married to the French chiropractor Serge Sautre, Paula is the mother of five children. The family lives in Atlanta, Georgia, U.S

Made in the USA
Columbia, SC
31 July 2021